Mount Clutter

Also by Sarah Lindsay
Primate Behavior

Mount Clutter

by

Sarah Lindsay

Grove Press
New York

Published simultaneously in Canada
Printed in the United States of America

FIRST EDITION

Library of Congress Cataloging-in-Publication Data

Lindsay, Sarah, 1958–
    Mount Clutter / by Sarah Lindsay.—1st ed.
        p. cm.
    ISBN 0-8021-3944-2
    I. Title.
PS3562.I51192 M68 2002
811'.54—dc21   2002067508

Grove Press
841 Broadway
New York, NY 10003

02 03 04 05   10 9 8 7 6 5 4 3 2 1

For Akira and Sachi Mizobuchi,

and for the ineffable Nora

Contents

The author wishes to thank George Bradley and Kay Ryan for advice and encouragement, Richard Howard for judicious attention to the manuscript, Joan Bingham and Zelimir Galjanic for help of all kinds, and Mickey McLean for tech support.

Grateful acknowledgment is made to the following publications, in which these poems first appeared: *The Antioch Review:* "Ice Hotel"; *The Atlantic Monthly:* "Laser Palmistry" (as "Laser Palmistry: The Early Years"); *Gloss* (www.glosszine.org): "House of Sand"; *The Kenyon Review:* "Morning on Despina," "Neoteny"; *The Paris Review:* "World Truffle"; *Pedestal* (www.thepedestalmagazine.com): "Mound Digger," "Slow Butterflies in the Luminous Field"; *Rhino:* "Caravan with Orchids and Pearls," "Olduvai Gorge Thorn Tree" (first place, Editors' Prizes); *River Styx:* "Guide to the Tomb of Ankhmahor"; *The Southern Review:* "Escape by Garbage, 1903"; *Southwest Review:* "Introduction of the Brown Tree Snake"; *The Styles:* "Hasselblad Meteorite"; *Tar River Poetry:* "Mount Clutter"; *The Threepenny Review:* Kirchfeld's Coffee," "Mawson's Pie."

I

House of Sand

Olduvai Gorge Thorn Tree

He kept dreaming of a tree, dreaming
of a tree, dreaming of a tree
and its sound like a hush,
and it seemed he could open
his mouth when he woke and make the others
know something they didn't already know,

his tree. But he woke and he couldn't.
He kept thinking of a tree. He made a tree
of his arms and called to the others,
but all he could say, all they could say,
was tree, not that one, no, not here,
tree. They were hungry, shrugged and went on.

Later a leopard dragged him some distance
and left him on the remains of his back,
his plucked face tilted up, and a seed
fell on the stub of his tongue
in his open mouth. Took root,
sent a finger between his teeth

that parted his jaws with its gradual thickness
and lifted its arms full of leaves that fed
on what was in his braincase
and mixed with the sky, and made
a sound in the wind that was
almost what he wanted.

Mount Clutter

One day when the planet was idly
pressing stegosaurs in her scrapbook,
she threw out a whole plateau
of souvenirs from the Ordovician, on impulse.
She'd long since run out of places to put things—
one reason these organelles are crammed into cells—
and naturally disorder breeds disorder:
you get distracted, you put down that scribbled
fossilized note about Martian microbes,
and once you set a tectonic plate on top of it,
you may never find it again. Though all kinds
of stuff will turn up while you're looking.

It's a realistic carelessness
that lets prize bones weather out of a cliff and crumble,
that shrugs when a secret cave on the coast,
with paintings of hands, great auks, and well-fed horses,
is sniffed out by the rough wet nose of the sea.
You can't expect your mother to save
your comic books forever, much less
her dried corsages,
snakeskins, pinecones, yearbooks, report cards,
and all the photo albums
from her life before you, on the chance
you might take an interest someday.

Be glad there's an attic, and a bunch of keys
that might fit something. Over here,
a sack of marbles she won off the neighbor boys, a sea-green
pillbox hat with a veil, a whole drawerful

of crinoids, a petrified forest, stromatolites . . . and here,
wrapped in the sports page from August third, 500 million B.C.,
it's the Cambrian worm *Insolicorypha psygma:*
dozens of bristles, a head divided in two,
if that was indeed the head. Once common as pennies;
now this is the only one. Go on rummaging,
brushing off dust, though you may find later
that it was the dust you wanted.

What if you don't find
the Missing Link, the Conclusive Proof
of that cherished hypothesis you cooked up
along with the instant soup on your hot plate
amid the books and shirts and notes and dishes?
Just see what she left you, without being asked:
opposable thumbs, cerebral cortex,
cuneiform, a recipe for piecrust,
and, in this shadowy corner, the rock itself,
prehistoric, prenotional Mount Clutter,
on which Occam's razor, like your inherited pocketknife,
is repeatedly wrecked and whetted.

Beethoven and the Ichthyosaurs
(Opus 135, Quartet in F major)

Beethoven hums three notes, "Must it be?" in his sleep.
Chaos theory has come to him in a dream,
but it won't be captured for another hundred years;
when he wakes it lingers only in his hair
and the distribution of little scars on his cheek.
It's hard to see a thing without a name.

Or with one. The fossils of the Lias epsilon layer
near Stuttgart looked like dragons at first, then stony fish,
then reptile fish imprinted on black slate.
For a while their spines were from sinners drowned
in the Flood;
later they became *Proteosaurus,* then *Ichthyosaurus communis,*
then *Stenopterygius quadriscissus,* poisoned by sulfurous mud.

On Beethoven's desk, a sheet of dust and light
obscures the motto framed under glass:
"No mortal can pierce My veil."
Delineate it, then. First, the viola,
grace notes, a groping march, lunge and stall,
scars rain down on the page black note by note.
Lento assai, cantate e tranquillo.

Five flats, then four sharps, clusters of vertebrae.
Slurred octaves, a waving tail that slows and stops.
Fallen black grains so faithful to a shape
that after a hundred million years you can trace its skin,
its unborn children, the record salted down
of what was and must be.

The Iguanodons of Bernissart, 1878

Three hundred twenty-two meters of honeycombed rock
down from the free air, a fall of gallery roof
sounds like a thousand doors slammed. Now all
De Pauw and his crew, trapped, can hear
is how aftersilence spreads around them,
stitched by slow dropping water. They are surrounded
by fallen compressed black inflammable
Carboniferous forest, except for this buried ravine,
lined with wet smelly black clay, whose bedded sands
they have harvested since May for dinosaur bones.
Here the Cretaceous toppled its junk.
In their small greasy light the woven bones,
pyritized, gleam like brass. But the lamps
must be extinguished. Now they hear themselves breathe.
De Pauw finds further speech too difficult:
words are so young in this place.

He came to Bernissart from the Brussels museum
with the engineer's telegram on the Saint Barbara mine.
Tearing out meters of sand in hopes of more coal,
the miners in the new gallery had pulled down pieces
of "something too black to be stone yet too hard to be wood,"
and when it split open it gleamed. Oh, let it be
tree trunks full of gold! No, Créteur
and most of the rest had seen iron pyrite before.
They knew its sickness, too, how easily it wastes
from fool's gold to gray powder.
But the manager sent the oddest pieces
to city scholars, and soon instead of coal
the miners mined iguanodons with De Pauw. This August day,

three hundred twenty-two meters up, tons of matrix
await their train, in plaster with bands of iron,
and the earth shakes, just a little.

Only a small tremor, only a little roof fell.
The work will continue—find out more, find more—
till Louis Dollo stands in the Brussels chapel
of George the dragon-slayer with one hundred twenty tons
of bony rocks to open and bones to nurse.
Bones dying their second death of pyrite disease
as they meet dry air. Forty lizards to save—
not counting the first one, chopped to bits in the mine—
by soaking each piece in alcohol suffused
with arsenic and shellac. No smoking allowed.
Try not to breathe much near the fume-hooded tanks. . . .
In the lasting night of the old rock forest,
De Pauw tries not to inhale the powder
articulating these remnants. What good is dust
to him if it holds no shape—he might as well
mine water, or air. How much air do they have?

Torn by his challenger's thumb spikes, the animal
leaves red drops as it blunders among the pines.
He's never been this far, doesn't know that the ground
opens wide here, and its lip crumbles under his foot
so he rolls hard to mud and stops hurting. Now he lies
near De Pauw, who shakes his head once, blankly,
when a grimy rescuer says it's only been hours.
The shaft disgorges him in time for supper.
Mere years later, after the first World War,

the Saint Barbara mine is abandoned to fill with flood.
In the Salle de l'Ère Secondaire of the Brussels museum,
iguanodons rear against their iron braces,
behind plate glass, like hollow kangaroos.
Professors hover on scaffolding near the faces
of still-decaying skulls too fragile to touch,
whose delicate gray contents go on forgetting.

Bone Hunters in Patagonia

Ostrich eggs and coffee, then a race to the sea's edge
that slides away from their camp every morning
over the dark green sandstone,
withdrawing like the future from their approach
to reveal this day's menagerie of old bones.
And as they stoop after the tidal skirts,
easing the itch of their hands on Nesodon skulls
and giant limbs of Astrapotherium,
the fog comes too, to close them in muslin rooms
about as wide as their reach. When they move
the mist moves with them, uncurling perhaps
from the small grinning jaws of a perfect Icochilus
or a Glyptodon dome figured with rosettes.
Set each treasure aside to find another
to set aside, still locked in its matrix,
to find another to set aside, and another, until
the water that yielded two miles of bony plain
begins to take it back. Now they shout
till the bluffs' echo tells them which way home;
they batter the unresisting cotton walls to find their prizes,
grunt and curse and heave the toothy blocks
with cool salt licking their heels. Save it all,
manhandle it past high water.
By evening the sea is music again,
ostrich-egg cakes are baking over the coals,
the green stones have been trimmed and laid out to dry.
This was science.
                    And this is history.
Hatcher and Peterson range along the tide
near Corriguen Aike all the Patagonian spring,

September–October 1896.
If the fog lifts for an hour they watch the grebes
bob on the surf, or porpoises
grin half-mammalian grins. More often
it muffles their sight, but faithfully bears their voices
from one to the other over half a mile.
Meanwhile the sailing ship *Columbia*
blunders sightless round the Horn
and wrecks near Port Desire. And half the Earth away,
Hatcher's wife sits by a small bed and writes,
beginning to be afraid. Their boy
is only three years, two months, and breathing hard.
Days later, he stops coughing.
She washes his soft hair. Nothing can hurt him now.
Hatcher, who will read of this in May,
is loading four tons of fossils for north Gallegos.
He has never seen such a wealth of species,
never been so happy.

Secrets of the Skoglund Shale:
The Auditorium Fossil

Thank you.
The discovery and preliminary excavation
        of deposits known as the Skoglund Shale
present scientists with what they love most:
        a solution to past mysteries
        that is itself mysterious.
I refer of course to the subject of tonight's lecture,
        Pseudoscarabaeus berglundi.

Portions of the creature have been known
        and misinterpreted for decades now.
Naturally, the most durable parts
        are most often found in the fossil record:
These rather beautiful hollow spirals,
        round or elongated,
        flared at one end, were discovered
in jumbles where currents had left them. Windus and Brown
        considered them shells
        of vanished soft-bodied sea creatures.

But as more of these spiral structures turned up
        in association with other forms—
straight tubes whose apertures were stopped
        with interconnected operculae—
Dimick, Malone, and Bretheim proposed
        a symbiotic model.
Only O'Dell and Breitag speculated
        that these might be remains of one large
        complex organism.

They were right. The Skoglund Shale
            is a book, when all we had before
            was alphabetic heaps. We see
complex cephalic organization,
strong bilateral symmetry,
a single ancient animal, roughly thirty meters long.

Note the level of detail in this specimen,
            preserved for us by chance.
The hornlike spirals are arrayed
            in the outermost layers of the head.
These, with several protrusions along one side,
            shaped like kettles, cylinders, sticks, and platters,
            must be its sensory apparatus.
The next row comprises the aforementioned tubes—
            siphons, perhaps, for underwater movement.

Now we come to a series of features
            never seen before:
at the base of the head, a conglomeration
            of hollow structures, crushed and splintered,
            bound each by three or four ligaments.
We find, furthermore, attached to each of these,
            and to each tube, and to each "horn,"
a highly articulated skeletal unit
            originally surrounded by soft tissue.

Of the thorax and abdomen there is less to say.
Note the clear line of the gut, like an aisle
            running straight down the middle.

On either side, fanning out like ribs,
        lie regular rows of plates, in right-angled
           pairs.
Approximately nine-tenths of these
        are associated with one skeletal unit apiece.
Oddly, similar plates appear in the head,
        perhaps displaced by the unknown cause
           of death
        or subsequent exposure.

Much though we need to learn from further study
        of *Pseudoscarabaeus berglundi,*
one can begin to imagine
        this strange organism in action
        a hundred twenty million years ago—
swimming, perhaps by rippling its armored body,
        in silence, near the floor of its shallow sea.
What did it eat? What did it have to fear?
We do not know. Indeed, we still await evidence
        of the number of legs, if any.
We're in no danger of running out of questions.

From its resemblance in many gross aspects,
        which you no doubt have noticed—
        horizontal orientation, tripartite form,
        rounded head, bilateral body—

one might rush to classify it
    as a somewhat larger, primitive form
    of our own modern beetles.
    (Hence the name.)
Let us for now, in the absence of stronger evidence,
    resist such hasty conclusions.
The facts we have are marvelous enough.

Hasselblad Meteorite

The Hasselblad floats from an astronaut's blubbery
1960s moon-shot gloves
and finds that it can fly, finds it can't stop,
and circles the homeworld, an unfocused eye
winking at pinpricks millions of light-years deep.

Scriptwriter A says that in 2089
that fateful camera, encrusted with star drool,
will hurtle from its decaying orbit and smite
the first immortal radioactive cockroach
on the brink of its unholy victory over the globe.
Squish.

What nonsense,
says Scriptwriter B. In 3010
it will immolate itself several miles
from the last immortal radioactive cockroach,
who leans in tears on the shoulder of her cello,
having broken the only remaining A string on Earth.

The camera's ash will lie peacefully in its crater
on fossilized seabed flecked with pale ancient spirals
just like the sky.

Mound Digger

This mound of dirt and the summer are hers to transfer
from what lies before to what lies behind,
pinch by pinch. Of the mound, she keeps a record.
The point, the students have been assured,
is not to find objects. Their object is
to understand the ground.
What water did with it, when.
How often earthworms combed and cast it.
Whether it was tilled or thrust aside,
which seeds lay in it, which pollens settled.

When it's too dark to dig, she makes a tent
of reading assignments. A chapter on similarities
between spear points unearthed in Virginia
and Solutrean points in Spain,
both kinds wrought as though for beauty
and cached in heaps of red ocher. Another book
invites her to peer at the keyhole shape of a bone
the size of her index finger, engraved
these ten thousand years with forty strokes—
fourteen, eight, eleven, then seven—and polished.

A tally, a game, the score?
We'll never know. And here's a review
of arguments about a broken rock
that might have been bashed into useful shape
deliberately, with another rock,
by some original axe-making biped,
or might be a geofact, a tease,

a found axe—or no tool at all.
She douses the light
and all the words disappear.

Morning, back to the mound. It's two mounds now;
she knows it halfway through, its wayward layers,
silky and barren or matted with nutrients,
heavy clay, a thousand shades of brown.
She sees it with her eyes shut, with her palms,
sometimes tastes it. Leave the flints and bones
to thrill-seekers and visionaries.
Dirt answers her questions. She has dug past
any props or plots or characters
to the stuff all stories walk on.

Kirchfeld's Coffee

He begins each class with a foam cup of the reconstituted
brown powder one calls coffee, and the next in a series
of cigarettes; as his students watch, fascinated,
he writes on the chalkboard behind him without getting up,
creates on the table before him a mess of chalk dust and ashes,
and transfers some to his necktie, some to his coffee,
lecturing all the while, or interrupting himself
with his dry uninflected laugh. In this room only the chalk
is capable of as many words as he is.

He knows the proper pronunciation of *rationale,*
cynosure, congeries (he chalks them behind him), yet
rumor says he came to English late, after Hungarian
and Latin, along with Russian, German, French, Greek,
        and something else,
all of which he speaks fluently, without accent.
Not that they've actually heard him. These undergraduates
grew up in jellied English like sprouts in agar.
They've never turned leaves of parchment from animals
skinned these eight hundred years, or stood in a library full
of a book written out on clay. One good earthquake
and it's so much grit; one good flood and it's paste.

All the books he owns now are curing themselves
        of immortality
with internal acids, turning tobacco-gold; in his dotage
each will be a heap of dust between covers.
Powdered language. He swallows what's in his cup,
still thirsty, always thirsty.

House of Sand

Living in this hourglass with the rest of us,
by now you may have noticed the dimple
forming in the center of the floor.
We can guess the outcome, but not the particulars.
Given any heap of grains,
the variables may be fewer than infinite,
but not by enough to do us any good.
No one has mastered the physics of sand,
not even with theoretical perfect spheres,
much less the real stuff—snowflakes being
the prettiest example, but cornflakes
are just as ornery settling down, or cinders.
Spill of salt, trickle of flour,
mound of sugar, hill of beans.
And don't forget the sly ways of dust.
Feed corn blows out the side of a steel silo
built to withstand mere gravity;
barley forms a moveless arch
just long enough for a puzzled farmer
to step inside and look up.
The Sahara's crawling muscles
boom at dusk; their low-pitched music
defeats notation, voice of the forces
that bloom in a dune or give it veins like lightning.
Shift, sift, avalanche, stasis,
no average behavior, no bell curve, no workable model,
but nothing so recognizable as disorder,
it's a pattern that, as you slide to the middle
bit by bit, you can never watch
long enough to understand.

Siberian Triangle

Given: We have received no signal.
Postulate: We should send one.
So thought Carl Friedrich Gauss,
who honored the property of density
by tending to have another idea
between any two ideas,
and in 1820 he proposed
an enormous, perfect right triangle,
hewn from Siberian forest and planted in wheat,
with a perfectly measured square on each side
grown up in pine trees for contrast.
Anything Out There sufficiently Euclidean
and responsive to visible light
would recognize, by whatever name,
the Pythagorean theorem,
and our existence.

Say it was done. Say
the germ of the plan infected a whole symposium,
one of whose members knew someone
who knew someone who brought it to
the attention of someone near the czar
who saw the glory of Russia in it
and snipped red tape with a wave of his hand.
Surveyors went out
with their one-eyed, three-legged instruments
and quivers of flags,
then farmers and foresters set to work,
plowing along the hypotenuse,
edging the squares with axes,

smitten with the idea of making
something pure and too big
to appreciate from the ground.

$a^2 + b^2 = c^2$
—for Gauss, the first language was mathematics.
A musician might have suggested acres
of C-major chord progressions, a chemist
symbolic formulas for water and carbon,
though either would take fancy plowing.
Anything but words; we want observers
to think of us as intelligent,
not idiosyncratic.
For years the triangular wheat field flourished,
the pines in their dark green quadrangles thickened,
and any passersby overhead might know
that although on an earlier pass
there was nothing to see
but bubbles in a swirl of hot sulfur,
we have mastered geometry.

But winter stayed late one year, and the next,
and pine logs fed the caretakers' fires.
Blight struck the wheat,
or perhaps the soil was exhausted;
a mottle of cabbage and potato patches
scabbed the right angle.
A path bisected segments AB and AC,
then iron tracks, punctuated with smoke
from short, cold trains.

Gauss and beings from outer space
amounted to less than silly rumors
to the gray men in the gray gulag
that was thrown together here,
a feature singularly ugly
from any vantage,
eventually abandoned.

The denizens of a concrete maze
spreading where pines used to grow
tell each other ghost stories and gossip,
having noticed, all their lives,
nothing more untoward in the sky
than the higher math of stars.
The field that was groomed
for an elegant equation
sends our muddled signal
not of order but of its fertile decay,
its outlines no more Pythagorean
than the patches mapped by water
on a towel, which the woman
who dried her hands now folds
to draw from her oven
a lump of good brown bread.

Mawson's Pie

Far to the north (but all food is north of here),
someone is eating potatoes
roasted in their jackets and gashed with butter;
someone is tilting a bowl
and letting cream roll down his throat.
Mawson wakes in the fuggy tent
from a dream of steak-and-kidney pie and tastes his blood;
his cracked lips are sealed with blood.

Mawson, David, Mackay, sunburnt, frostbitten, hungry.
They could stay in their bags and let the magnetic pole
walk over them on its unmapped course.
They could take three steps outside and vanish
into another crevasse just like the one
where Mawson dangled in harness, waiting for rescue,
noted the pure color of its bottomless sides,
and tossed up ice crystals for study.

They fold away their teabag to use again.
They carefully catch and eat the crumbs from their biscuits.
Walking on ice that is every wrong shape for their feet,
they come at last to a place where the compass needle
stands up straight between them. Each has
saved the others' lives, and bored them
near death with his stories. Here
they look at each other like strangers.

Then they start back. They speak of hot coffee with milk,
lamb chops, buttermilk, treacle pudding.
The pole, relinquished, drifts another inch,

and crevasses in all directions open lipless mouths.
Far to the north,
sailors lost in the southern ocean
and starved for landfall take as their guides
wide-winged seabirds that may never fly to shore.

Escape by Garbage, 1903

Rotten peas and penguin blood,
spoiled dried fish and coal ash.
As the Antarctic days grow lighter,
the ship's crew rakes out all its dark garbage
across the ice, a dirty carpet spread
from the ice-locked vessel to open water
six hundred meters away.
Drygalski, ship's geologist,
thinks if they blacken the ice they might make it thaw.
At least it's too cold to smell.

A century earlier, Carl Friedrich Gauss
without leaving his study ascended to the height
from which he set on Earth's damp skin
his paired marks, like a phrenologist's fingertips,
for geodetic measurement.
This is the thin mental altitude of infinitesimal calculus,
quadratic residues, lemniscate functions,
the proof of the impossible.
From here the planet is a small but gallant sphere,
bearing a pure white shield without device.

Borne up by the only hot air for miles,
Drygalski rises in the ship's balloon to the end of its tether
and—of course—looks down. White silence, clarity
almost like mathematics. The ship
is covered with ice, like everything else in sight
except the hill where they found their first solid rock.
One hawser, one line, of the kind

that assumes its true form only in Euclid,
ties Drygalski to Carl Friedrich's desk:
a name. The hill is Gaussberg, their ship the *Gauss*.

With his newly invented heliotrope,
Gauss turned to the sun, and enmeshed the land
in focused lines of light.
With only a pair of compasses and a straightedge,
he inscribed a heptadecagon in a circle.
He wandered into non-Euclidean numbers,
but his writing hand faltered. There, perhaps,
parallel lines met; there his proof of the impossible
could be disproved. Irrational and rash.
He put those papers away.

For weeks the spring sun shines on the trash
and makes it mushy. Little pools join in a trough
that becomes a shallow channel
that drinks December's surprising rain. In February,
two jolts and the trap gives way. Foghorns and gunfire
bring the last men scurrying back from the ice,
and the *Gauss* embarks on a crooked path
into a non-Euclidean century.
Under its keel a strange filthy rain
falls through the sea whose shield no longer holds.

Introduction of the Brown Tree Snake

The trees fill with silk, and the space between trees,
white canopies clotted with insects,
cones and tunnels of silk
that lead to the weavers, eight-legged pouches
with clusters of ruby eyes.
Their work is no longer undone by midmorning—
torn by geckos or trailed from the wings
of fantails, flycatchers, fruit doves, and honeyeaters.
A tree snake leaves the weft intact
as it drinks from a broken egg at midnight
or settles at dawn with a lizard in its throat.

A thousand tree snakes barely displace the night
more than the two or three, five or six or nine
that unwound from the machinery
of a couple of troopships fifty years ago,
fitted their lengths to the island beach,
and narrowly tasted the air. Now the stories
make endless chains: I left the bar
and my first four steps, I stepped on four snakes,
this big around. I woke to a tug;
it was pulling, its fangs through my nostril.
She whelped five puppies, but an hour later
just one was left. I ran to the nursery
and found two snakes in the crib.

Her first night on the island, he takes her hunting
with flashlights, for a preliminary count.
A six-footer woven through cyclone fence. Another.
She stumbles, although the lawn

is perfectly flat, perfectly mowed.
The honeyeaters are gone, the rufous fantails,
the flycatchers, the fruit doves; that much is known.
The last brown rails live indoors.
Geckos, skinks—uncertain. Brown tree snakes
can grow to be nine feet long.
Plum-size spiders now build cooperative webs.

Those that succeed repel us, she thinks.
(Another. Twenty, twenty-one.) If lizards
infested our houses, every one chewing eight black legs,
would I shudder at their reptilian eyes
and the tiny scales on their toes? If fat birds
studded the lawns, eviscerating the last of the snakes,
would I tend a snake colony, count the snake babies,
admire the pink satin lining of their mouths?
Beyond the little puck of her flashlight
the veiny dark is moving.
She opens her mouth to say
There's another one, forty-eight,
and a thread breaks over her lips.

The Common Fruit Fly

Five hundred generations
since we traced the sweetness above a windfall apple.
Instead we taste your scheduled anesthesias
and wake on a shelf in flasks to be filled
with our stubborn procreation.
You pour us out on Mondays.
You sort us with thick fingers.

We are the white-eyed, the red-eyed, the eyeless,
with full wings, with crumpled vestigial wings.
We perceive the buzz of fluorescence you call quiet,
its flicker you call light.
The chemical stream of your midafternoon banana
sings behind our mouthparts.
We are the tested.

We stir at sunrise and rest in time with sunset
in a lab without a sun. We repeat the courtship rites
of our grandfathers and grandmothers and their
great-great-great-great-great-great-great-great-
grandparents, and our desire is roused
and quenched as though
you were not watching.

You seem to relish our otherness—
protruding honeycomb eyes, hooked hovering bodies—
but spend your tenure measuring only
the ways we are like you. We turn to light,

we hunger, we flinch from shocks and avoid their source.
We exhibit not only response to pain
but memory of pain.

Unless you take memory, too.
Your hands and voices flourish
when you prove that the piece you subtracted from our cells,
or bestowed on the cells of our young, controls a trait,
and you can make us blind or clever or amorous or clockless.
Knowledge must be sweet.
May we taste it?

Slow Butterflies in the Luminous Field

In this kennel you'll see our most popular cross:
golden retriever with Red Delicious apple.
The apple genes make 'em glossy and calm
and symmetrical. They travel well,
don't jump, don't run around, don't bark.
Frankly, we didn't expect their teeth
to be so soft, but they do just fine on mush.
Handsome, aren't they?

                              Down that hall
are miniature poodles with parrot genes,
bright blue with yellow eyes. The night shift
taught this batch to say Help! I'm being held prisoner
in a fortune-cookie factory!
It was funny the first hundred times.

This room will be for hamster turtles.
The pet stuff may not change the world,
but we can't do that without income, right?

Now in this paddock we're saving the rhino
by making it woolly again. With vicuña genes,
it's relatively docile, it's fluffy, lots of square footage—
mark my words, rhino fleece will be hot.
And look at those Bambi eyes—who goes on safari
to shoot a cream puff like this?

Most of our projects are in development.
In here we're working with kudzu genes in silkworms
to increase the output and tensile strength,

but so far we've only doubled their appetite.
And the spider-barnacle thing has yielded
intriguing results, but nothing we're ready to publish.

But out here—you should see this field in the evening
when we let the butterflies out.
Looks like ordinary tobacco, doesn't it,
but those leaves are making insulin as we speak.
We also incorporated a jellyfish gene.
That's for the butterflies, which are part slow loris—
that way they can't start hurricanes by fluttering,
or migrate to where their forests used to be.
When the butterflies turned out nocturnal too,
we figured we'd make the tobacco plants glow in the dark.

At night they give off a pale green light,
and bow their heads, from a bluebell cross, I think,
to be pollinated more easily,
and the butterflies walk in slow motion up the stalks.
Their wings open and close every minute or so;
maybe they think they're flying. And the plants
move their leaves a little, too,
as if they were shifting in a summer breeze,
as if there were any more breezes.

Laser Palmistry

Determined not to ask too much,
the chiromantic surgeon's very first client
passed up the lottery-winning star along the Apollo line,
the peacock's eye on the Mercury finger for luck
     and protection.
But, given the discount for scientific advancement,
she made four choices: erase the ring of Saturn
that circled her left middle finger and kept her melancholy;
build up her mount of Apollo, to make her
lively and creative; lengthen her heart line—
she would be discriminating and faithful in love;
and draw her a good strong fate line, because she had none.
What kind? "Surprise me," she said,
opened her hands, and felt so naked
she had to close her eyes.

Who knew that while his meticulous lasers worked,
the tea leaves in her mug in the kitchen sink
shifted before they dried? Or that, three counties over,
a sheep suffered cramps as its entrails readjusted?
Meanwhile, no fewer than nine unrelated people
felt tickles like ants in their palms as their own lines moved.
That night, while the patient's unexpected headache
accompanied minor changes in the protuberances of her skull,
a few widely scattered astronomers frowned
at anomalies in their data,
and on Floreana, in the Galápagos Islands,
an as yet undiscovered vein
of perfectly aligned crystals disappeared.
And that was just the beginning.

II

Discovery of the
Bufo Islands

A Map of the Bufo Islands

At the end of any triple batch of cookies,
one sheet goes into the oven sparsely knobbed
with mismatched lumps of bowl scrapings,
liable to be forgotten and overbaked.
These are the Bufo Islands, too small
and bloodless for any proper atlas
but so designated on this antique, anonymous map.

On the Flinders chart, on the other hand,
the same configuration and number of spots
has wandered 2 degrees, 10 minutes west
and answers to King Philip III of Portugal Islands.
The Hiebenstreidt chart
shows nothing in either place.

Are they a family, wherever they lie—
stitched together by seed-bearing bats
with the ghost-wedge faces of possums,
or related by the flavor
of their fundamental stone? Or were they bound
only by the decision of some untraveled,
constellation-hungry geographer?

Each has been named too many times
to have a name. Men in outriggers
called them after a bird, a weather,
a lack of sweet water;
men in sailing ships and coal-burners
named them through glass for sponsors, monarchs,
sweethearts, or themselves.

No one, we think, stayed ashore. No humans
looked for the only living population
of the ancient opabinia—five eyes, groping nose—
or recognized the voice of the four-toed sloth.
They sailed on, seeking diamonds and nutmeg,
water and meat. And couldn't have found
these bumps again had they tried.

It was only
the world's six vestigial tailbones that they passed.
Cracked accidents of dough.
The usual bland tips of sea-shrouded mountains,
a few bits of sleep crusted
in a volcano's eyes.

Aiaia

This tooth of land is old, old,
weathered down to a nub and the nub weathered down.
Humans trying to sleep here
would find no curves that fit their bodies.
Older than its place in the sea
is Aiaia, connected series of itself,
last remaining piece of the Earth egg's perfect shell
that cracked on the third day
and never was smooth again.

The planet wetted its surface with exhalations,
and shards of the Ur-continent,
burned and plowed by meteorites,
began their rearrangement. Aiaia
was polar, equatorial, continental, isolate,
baked and frozen, washed, collided with,
and always wandering. Its rooted speed
seemed slow only to the latecomer algae,
anemones, and jawless fish that wiggle and falter faster.

Its crust and shoals accumulated beings:
Crinoids and jellies softly touched it,
ammonites saw it with newly invented eyes.
It was cool enough for the bellies of gasping lungfish,
warm enough for scurriers in sparse fur;
its thermals lifted bats
on the extravagant fabrication of their wings.
The five-eyed, claw-nosed Cambrian opabinia
here, as nowhere else on Earth, neglected to die out.

These days Aiaia sails separated
by a deep-sea rift from the rest of the Bufo Islands,
sharing their white-faced fruit bats
but without a single toad.
A few sea turtles bump against its shore
where their memory sees open water; whales go around.
Chapped earth cakes the stony base,
and the plants that feed on it, new to the wind,
taste of age, a sour garlic tang.

All seems still. But the island grinds in its bowels
a few small diamonds, and bones of pygmy elephants;
insects pluck and twang its particles,
fallen leaves fur it with fresh decay—
and in the tide pools on its most broken side,
a luminous protozoan makes a pale blue spot in shadow.
If a molecule near its heartless center ticks left,
it will become an animal; if not, a plant. For now,
it wallows in inches of water, young
as an egg on the third day, glowing with indecision.

Neoteny

Unlike tadpoles, big-eyed and wiggly,
or bat babies with snub puppy faces
and skins of helpless velvet,
the island was born
red-faced and belching, hunchbacked, shifty,
sharp, and hot all over.
Nothing about it in infancy
would endear it to a mammal mother,
move her to coo and keep it safe.

The white-faced bat feeds her three-day-old,
which fortunately resembles a teddy bear;
she can tell it by smell from a hundred others
bundled inside their hollow tree; she is drawn
to this one as if it were joy.
And by more than coincidence, we must suppose,
she learns indifference to it about the time
it grows as big as she is and sprouts
a mournful horse-skull muzzle just like hers.

The young bats fly off
to give our nightmares something to fix on—
the pitiless way it stared at me without recognition,
the pitiless way it flew right at my head and missed,
the pitiless way it flickered in circles above me
as if I weren't there—
and we hold our babies tight, for consolation.
Soon they will be too big to cry out
without giving a reason.

The tads are warty and baggy now,
and long white faces on grown-up wings
ride over fruit trees, over the straits.
But the island in its maturity
has gone soft and rounded, pink and green,
as it swallows the bones of their mothers.

Morning on Despina

Lioness morning falls on Despina.
The island shrinks in the heat.
Warmed, the caterpillars in green heaps uncurl,
disengage, take up their threads,
and file back to their round.
And round and round. Each follows the silk
of the one before and leaves a trail
for the one behind. Head to end,
hungry but unresisting, they march.
The tender pegs of their feet in thousands
dot the dirt as they go.
A ribbon of silk, a growing rampart of silk,
in a nearly perfect circle rims Despina.

The four-toed sloth is too nearsighted to see it.
Inland, she hangs from an ancient tree covered
with young leaves, some of which she digests, upside down.
Her long soft hair parts over her belly;
green things grow in it. To her they smell sweet.
Nothing goes on happening,
like her own heart lazily squeezing its juice
in the Gothic arch of her nearly uncrushable ribs.
She hums. It's easy not to stop—
long notes, round as her browless head,
many as leaves on this branch she can't see the end of,
where so far today she has unhooked one foot
and hooked it again, a little farther along.

The bat dismisses that sound.
What she can't hear is the other bats,
flown to Corbett for cottonfruit
while she stays with a late baby pinned to her chest.
She pops the skin of an unripe lungberry;
sour juice pinches her tongue. What she almost hears
is the python, bunched where shade lies deep,
shivering to warm her eggs. The bat hangs herself up,
a sloppy brown cone of wings with a horse-skull face.
Her little one mews. She pictures the snake—
peristalsis of a nearby branch—
and her baby lost, her baby safe. On all Despina,
only she sees the divisions of forked life coming.

A Walk on St. Agnes Island

Call it St. Agnes Island; somebody did.
But no one comes here. Its salient feature
is brownness. Machete-proof forests
of low knotted trees take into their arms
parasitic figs that bind them to earth,
and both feed a filmy brown fungus.
The flying squirrels, leaf monkeys, barking deer
probably would have been brown anyway,
but when so much of the rest was brown,
everything had to be—
the shy brown spider, the snake, the lizard
pretending to be a stick, even the small round butterflies
tilting their wings to the sun on slack lips
of flowers that bloom sienna, umber, fawn.

And the toads, of course: one kind an inch long,
springing in sudden dozens away
from your heavy feet like splashing water,
others deep in the shade that grow large
as cannonballs and speak with cannon voices.
Walk carefully here in the headless grass
that grows in loops like croquet wickets;
you might be stepping on toad bird snake mud
cricket mantis moss or shrew or just grass.
It whispers underfoot, behind your back,
but all it says is *brown.*

The guabe guabe takes more and more
of the ground the grass wanted. It's not a grass
or a shrub or mushroom, just mealy brown fingers

poking up everywhere, crumbling the dirt,
impinging on beaches, leaning over streams.
Nothing eats it. No one knows
that if sun ever fell on its roots they'd prove to be
snow-white and violet, rose and mauve—
they hide with the roots of the stunted trees
that branch in tangles sixty feet down
with sapphires in their hair.

Here the air is a faint brown
from the volcano's plume that stains the horizon,
and if you stumble at dusk and put out your hands
it could be leaf mud petal or wing
pressed tender against your palm, it could be
a pouch of toadskin that feels like yours
without temperature, drawn taut over a pulse
and barely holding it in.

Corbett Island

If you were there
you might feel a thread of something on your arm,
nothing you could see, and another.
Later your hand, brushing off that nothing touch,
might roll up a little green remnant with legs.
Later the sun might catch one on your knee
so you'd see it, transparent, green, with big pale eyes,
wings crested high on its back.
The sun and the labor of newness might put you to sleep
among all the things you'd never seen,
and they've never seen one like you,
but they land on you lightly once you're there:
elbow crease, thumb web, eye tuck.
A good moist salt they've found and more keep coming.
A shape like yours lies over you
made of tiny transparent scales.
They fly away glistening, leave you dry.
You're gone. But every single one
of your visitors will have a thousand children.

To Be an Island

The fur snake cranes its neck, which is its body,
and swivels, but nothing is watching, so
it lowers and laps. Its small sharp teeth
are good at opening eggs and the softer parts
of its mousy kin. About two feet long,
fawn-colored, a kind of legless weasel,
it doesn't eat much, sleeps a lot,
likes to take its slender helping of sun
on a high branch the width of its back.
It likes to wake and stretch so thoroughly
its flat nose wrinkles.

With rough bare skin on its belly, and practice,
it hardly ever falls. And nothing lives here
that has a taste for it, or jaws
to shake it to rags—nor are there snakes
to shame its imitation. It will
get better at what it does,
like the marsupial hedgehog, like the stumpy flightless bird,
because they live on an island. They have time.

To be an island, you have to stand back from the others,
drawbridge up. That way you get
to have your own ideas. You can share—
send out your bats, your golden dancing midges
(*D. wiederhoefti*), certain waterproof seeds;
let the whiskerfish come over, and Owen's gull
with its raucous trombone honk, even
a couple of stubborn elephants, strong swimmers,

if their children agree to stay small,
eat less, give up their favorite foods.
But be wary of gifts.

That way lie rats and roaches, goats and mosquitoes,
everything that feasts upon
the tender and slow. That way you get grackles
and sparrows, not that they don't have their place,
instead of the bird with short green wings,
magenta head, and snowy breast,
that bears in four years
just two rusty young.

And you have to gamble.
You *are* a gamble—numbers rule,
and their feckless godmother, chance.
The pygmy elephant population dwindled,
but might have managed an upward turn
when there were fifty left, if the youngest female
hadn't sickened and died. Of the merest scratch.
But during a drought, the Lothar palms survived
because four baseball seeds fell late
and rolled just far enough to drop
into the last wet cleft.

Even when the ocean shrank
and several islands, north by northwest,
woke up all one country, the island Aiaia
kept its moat. It missed out on the humming sloths,
but upheld its fur snakes. Every inch is alive,

full of mistakes and the ones between,
its pondwater paisley under a lens, its plainest dirt
tremulous with microbes. Lothar palms
in dozens nod their crowns of arms,
drinking with thrifty roots the last
of the pygmy elephants' marrow.

Amphibious

Not for the first time,
it shrugs from the sea, inconstant, nameless,
chill skin over a bubble of heat from the deep.
Its kelpy hair lies down streaming, tangled
with startled barnacles, squirming shrimps,
shark teeth, little squid rolling downhill while they can,
and torn wings of fish whose jewel colors
fail as they rise.

Its topknot of grass
indifferently drinks either salt or sun,
but the brick velvet puckered around the grass dies in the air.
A black velvet slowly takes that place, and thrives,
patted by salamander feet. Bats in passing
drop cottonfruit seeds into richness. Toads
in their season pock new mud with their bellies
and lift up their voices.

But the whaleback island
bows again. Sea folds readily over it,
breaking the ribs of skinny fruit trees.
Mako cabbages sail away, turning their heads without necks.
Salamanders sprout soft antler gills.
Deflated toads part from their egg-strung weeds,
whose loose arms, twirled inside out, shake off
jelly-pearl bracelets.

An octopus
feels its way into a newly wet cave.
A haze of triangular flies hangs over

the rumpled waves, waiting for someplace to land,
but the white-faced bats, hearing water beneath them,
fly on to Corbett. The flooded grass blushes blue-green
and puts on brick velvet for the next few days or centuries,
unable to drown.

On the Horizon

The island that draws me on
lies ahead where the curved ocean falls away,
my constant mirage, my ray of light,
I its point of intersection.

That one is my desire, the deed undone,
not the one whose sand I'll gash with my prow,
not the spiny hunk of mud that falls
when I open my clenched hand.

The shore I see is the beautiful one,
with trees of green glass,
a symmetry of animals, mist I can walk on
lit from within.

In the diagram of delusion,
I too am smooth and simple, black and white,
and a dotted line of nails flies from my eye
to tack my dear to the air till I arrive.

Thoughts on an Island

We haul our boat between the frontal lobes,
climb their wrinkled humps, and say,
"We're on the island." Never *in.*
But it's not just a lump on a stalk in the water—
see, it extends, a drafty cylinder
of interrelation, above us.

Just over our heads, in the thickest part of night,
white flowers sweeten and loosen
as sickle-nose bats lean in.
They know each other's time; they wake for each other.
After an hour bruised satin falls,
and the bats flicker home to lick their sugary faces.

Just over our heads, in the broadest sun,
green flies dance in a translucent whine.
Eat drink eat drink eat drink they must be singing,
their mouthparts formed for eating and drinking only,
yet they seem to do nothing but bob in the heat
like so many threadless needles.

Then of course there are birds. We know them as certain
capable bodies with beaks and wings, but we see them
as streaks—a one-second bar of magenta or lemon—
between two trees. We assign to them
any piercing cries and most of the uninflected racket
that passes for silence here.

But higher still, the gulls are passing
yet never past, wheeling, moveless,
as if they are stars to steer by, as if
they are fixed and we are shifting beneath.
Sometimes we believe them—until they blat,
fold into mere selves, and drop.

Above them, on cloudless days,
there is nothing, we say—
we who can't even see air.

Barbie on the Beach

Sand itself washed up first,
crushed in the sea's mill, ground in fish gizzards.
A beach at last, the beach began collecting:
battered jellies, reeking cartilage, boas of seaweed,
shells, mostly. A clam family's broken dishes.
A disproportionate number of left-handed spirals.
But not one human footprint, so, after centuries of wrack,
it's called pristine.

No people come to this island, no ship sails near.
The ocean shuffles and deals.
The sand acquires a bicycle pedal, a football,
cloudy bottles drained of Egyptian beer and Japanese whiske
And just above the line of high tide, with a few
    left-handed whelks,
Barbie stands, at a half-risen angle,
one arm missing, high-heel hooves embedded,
old-style face imperishably severe.

Her hair, turned a kind of caramel green,
and what was left of her dress are woven elsewhere
into a reedy cup around two speckled eggs.
Brown stuff grows in her joints, and a puddle
lives inside her torso.
Imperiously her remaining arm
lifts the back of her hand to the sky;
a crab sidles under its palm, but hurries away.

The tucked red flower of her lips
is flaked and pale, but her molded lashes
are still black, and her slant unclosing lids.
Day after voiceless day, she outstares the sun.

First on Clooney

Surrounded by singing indifference
on land where the map shows naked ocean,
you think you have discovered this place
till you find the charred stones
of your predecessors' fire. Would you settle
for being *their* discoverer?
Why does the air now enter your lungs less keenly?

You can't be the first to sight the Bufo Islands,
the first to land on St. Agnes or Corbett. You can
be first to set foot on Clooney or Lesser Clooney.
       What am I bid?
Pardon? All right then, first white guy
who keeps a log in an occidental language
and lives to tell about it. We'll call this
the first *recorded* landing. Twenty-five, thirty-five, fifty,
sold! to the pallid gentleman with the cane,
for three months' seasickness, most of his toes,
and a lasting inability to bear large crowds.
Now, first to describe the fauna, what am I bid?

You could be first to publish concerning
the Bufo sloth's fourth toe, and peculiarities
in its facial musculature and appendix, thereby
establishing that it is a separate species. You could
name it after your beloved wife, who's home
with the two-year-old son you haven't seen yet.

Next, the honor of being the one to determine
whether it spread to Clooney from Despina
or the other way round. No one? Right,
we'll send in our own fanatics to mop up as usual.

What's that? How much to be second? Sorry,
we don't handle that, sir; not much call for second.
But plenty of items left, ladies and gents,
for discriminating tastes: first black, first woman,
first black woman, first octogenarian—
who keeps track? why, you do, of course—
first to climb Dissension Peak;
that ought to get you a mention in any
thick history of this area. Proof? You'll find
you don't need it after awhile.

Management takes no responsibility
for any fading of the glorious flush
you feel on first beholding your prize
and striding to it in confident boots,
or for any melting or settling in shipment
of the limited-edition snowflakes auctioned this morning.
They were beautiful, weren't they?

Hanging Rock

The pyramid of Cheops, upside down.
A towering family tree with heavy branches,
teetering on the balding head
of a single son and heir.
A Paleolithic figurine,
radiant with significance
increased by the number of missing others—
her face a blank, her pubic triangle
carefully incised, her body a wedge
that tapers from broad shoulders to the point
where her legs end without feet.

At the best of times, the piti's characteristic call
dropped a melancholy third from its bright beginning.
But the last live piti in all the islands
has made no sound for days.
Taken into captivity, she laid a single sterile egg
and fell silent. The project interns, respectfully hushed,
watch the aviary in shifts.
Sometimes she hops, or tilts her head,
opens her long beak with its unusual flanges
and closes it again. It doesn't take much
to dry up an isolate gene pool, or puddle—
build a few towns where there were trees,
bring in some rodents and snakes. Island species
are often flightless, or nearly: The strongest fliers,
the adventurous, disappeared over the sea;
the timid ones stayed and passed on their diffident genes.
Now, at the base of the mountain, uneaten fruit

deposits the seeds too close to the tree.
From her sketchy nest in a glass house, the piti
regards a piece of mango.

Hanging Rock was a mounded peak,
then a pillar whittled in a rush of water,
worn to a flat-topped hourglass
left nakedly dry for air to scour.
All over the world, these top-heavy balancing acts.
All over the world, the dust of their collapse.
It blows across the space between rain and river
in the same wind that bears up birds that have flown so long
their descendants will have no feet.

Ameldonia

If we are blessed,
as we have been blessed before,
sullen colors are smudging the night
where a patch of ocean boils and splits,
where no one goes, yet.

For a long time the Bufo Islands went undiscovered;
then for years they were known to be unknown.
Sailors passed them
looking for drinking water and naked women,
not salamanders or scrubby brown trees
or four-toed sloths embroidered with algae.

One or two lay down there and died
with green flies walking their collarbones.
But wandering contrarians caught the islands' siren song:
Don't come here. Don't build a hut or look for gems,
don't find out fur snakes taste like pheasant,
don't tear up guabe guabe roots for dye.
Let the names you give us evaporate when you go.

Discoveries rained on the first explorers,
were wrung out by the last.
Lothar palms came down with sounds of gunfire and surrender.
Silverweed crept in somehow and grew
to strangle the cottonfruit. Graduate students in labs
observed the single-celled creature behind the legend
that Aiaia's coast glowed at night.

But possibly in the opposite ocean
flotsam finds a new mooring place
on shrugging lava shoulders.
One morning the first inhabitant
makes grudging landfall: eight hot feet
on the stone of a new Krakatau.

Life stumbles in as usual, off course,
adapted to bewilderment,
resolved to take advantage.
A bird that calls *a part, a-part, apart,*
gray-blue grass and orange lichen,
moss with seasonal horns.

On the Bufos, we approach comprehensive knowledge
by covering half the distance to it, half the remaining distance,
half the diminished remnant, half again.
The pleasure of leaping subsides into the achievement
of ever finer filigree along one edge of Darwin.
Half-inch ripples from a cataclysmic rising
on the other side of the world wash up unnoticed.

A ship steams away with a box of treated skins.
Someone has nailed a "flying possum"
by its open wings to the side of a Quonset hut.
Now come the settlers, who love recognizing
known smells and noises, the daily worn path,
who say to the land, "Don't change, don't ever change,"
as they sink the piles for their houses.

But if we are blessed, the pressure on this incognita
has raised one elsewhere.
We'll call it Ameldonia, "mother of the world,"
when we resume our delighted orgy of naming;
it will surprise us, may survive us,
might even save us. With every new name, loss.
With every new thing, mystery.

III
Changes

Orpheus Tries Again

Don't sing, this time, to the three-headed dog.
They'll know it's you by the crack in your voice,
sneaking in again. Rules are rules
down there, and "lost love" means "you had your chance."

Walk softly in the stunted wood
whose leafless trees are bodies of the dead,
through which the frail spirits wander, alert
to any disturbance, any sound or scent.

No coffee before you go, then,
no bacon or fresh bread. Wash three times,
yourself and all your clothes, but avoid the odor
of soap and towels; use only air to dry.

Leather holds your scent: no shoes.
Whatever you do, don't go near cigarettes.
Some say it helps to rub your feet and hands
with year-old sage or rind of pomegranate.

Don't brush the stiff dark arms
you walk between. Set your feet one and one.
It may be or seem days before you find her.
Don't sleep; don't sit down.

There she is. Hold still.
As long as she doesn't know, you can watch the shift
of thought to feeling to thought. A sigh, a turn.
Not much, but it's her; it's different from the script

of your finite set of memories.
Breathe shallowly. If you don't cry, you might get
two minutes of your beloved doing nothing
before you start to sweat.

Turn Us into Trees

Turn us into trees, they said,
holding hands, blushing a little
before the bemused immortals. *After we die,*
let us not be divided or human.

The thunder god and his messenger,
playing hobo on Earth to escape from boredom,
grew hungry, but found no welcome except
from the aging couple in the poorest one-room house.
Invited to dine, the strapping deities
hunkered down at a makeshift table, trying to follow
discourse on mathematics and travel
and making up answers to lots of friendly questions.
She poured out the last of the olive oil
and her husband called her beautiful;
he stood to carve their only goose
and she gazed at him as if he were Achilles.

So Zeus and Hermes unveiled themselves
and offered the world, and this was the mortals' request
of the storm god with a history of briefly loving
anything soft that moved, and the thief
who knew, laughed at, possibly authored
every sad story of squandered wishes
that ended with hair sold for watch fobs
or a sausage stuck to a nose.
Sobered by such constancy and willingness
to stay in one place, the noisy god
and the lightfoot lightfingered god released these two
from the Fates. And threw in a couple of geese.

Time passed, almost enough, not enough.
They were ready. She drew his cot outside
with his jaundiced, lightening body. He let out his breath.
She saw his eyes film with sky. "Sweet man."
She drifted along his side and touched his face,
then felt wind lift her arms,
wind under her hair, in her mouth.
"Dear love," said her mouths
that were also her hands and hair
shaken out by wind.
She bowed, he bowed,
they began forming rings for each other.

The breezes brought them traveling air
that knew similar stories—crinoids in shale
whose hardened shapes were Precambrian valentines,
bristlecone pines a canyon apart
that grew toward each other an inch every hundred years,
a pair of cathedral trunks in a rain forest
offering up bromeliad cups of water,
red miro trees on a coral atoll
with nothing to feed their roots but their own fallen leaves,
two oaks on Elm Street reaching arch-wristed
to touch across four lanes of traffic,
the steepled red rose and the briar. . . .

But also the lightning strike, bark strips peeled
from steaming wood. Slow galls and cankers,
beetles under the skin. Extraction whole,
like molars, from sodden ground. Or simply

ripe old age and decay. They didn't ask
for eternity, only years of brushing together.
She tosses him olives; he combs her hair. They scatter
seed endearments in a circle around their feet,
and each that sprouts
will age to sow its own circle,
till the continent is covered with slow-blooming rings
like a pond in rain.

In the Hall of the Double Axe

Before he reached the charnel heart of the maze,
but long after he would have lost his way
without the thread in his hands, he stopped
in muttering irritation: another
snarl in this so-called skein, this blob,
to pick out before it would go on unspooling;
a princess and her handmaids you'd think
could do neater work than this.

He sat decisively on the earthen floor
where a cul-de-sac on one side widened the passage,
to see the thing done right. He unwound it all—
full of slut's-wool, splinters, and insects
as if the length had been dragged across
an untended floor like this one—down
to the inner end and a half-moon clove of garlic
like the one she hung on his neck.

He hadn't thought there would be so much of it
heaped and kinked around him, smelling
of lemon and cedar like her clothes,
twisting where it lay. Rough lengths
of grassy rope that snagged
on his calluses were awkwardly knotted
to yards of fine red silk, or stuff
that might be a woman's hair.

A sailor of sorts, he could make better splices
to unreel smoothly. He set to work,
picking out thistles, strengthening weak spots,

beginning to roll up a proper balanced ball.
In part of his mind meanwhile he invented
a gadget for winding and unwinding quickly,
perhaps an improved technique for spinning thread.
He started to whistle, but stopped.

The pile of culled beetle shells and dead spiders grew.
From time to time, rumor of the
presence in the labyrinth's center
shook the cyclopean walls, even at that distance.
He raised his face and absent eyes
at the sound, stretched his shoulder muscles,
flexed his fingers, then bent again
with pleasure to his task.

Changes

The fields of discovery then were barely furrowed,
overgrown with stories. Philosophers
knew all the science there was. One of them—
Democleitus, Antimedes, some such pebbly name—
after years of moveless labor spoke.
"Poets are blind," he said. "They sing
one half and miss the other. The cosmos
is and must be perfectly balanced;
metamorphosis, beloved of tale-spinners,
requires its compensation."

For every marble statue made sweet flesh
for its smitten maker, a woman somewhere
turns to stone. If blood, accidentally spilled,
rises from trampled dirt as red petals,
another flower's veins are lopped open,
shedding ichor. And when the old couple
who prayed to be never parted
became two trees, entwined, with green years ahead,
two young people woke in a forest
in puzzled embrace.

King Midas stroked the pelt of a meadow
and made a heavy yield of gold blades,
but over the mountain, dry grass greened
and took up its whispered tale. The hero
Jason sprouted a thousand soldiers
from dragon's teeth, but across the sea
a thousand soldiers, breathing fire,
fell in a swamp's wet coils.

The goat-god played his new flute by the water.
A reed cried out in the hills and found
it was a woman's throat. And for all the pursued
and fleeing women enclosed at the very last moment
in bark and cambium, others awoke
for the first time with leaves in their hair—a replacement
sufficient for natural law, if not for
the thwarted lovers, not for the women themselves.

When the seven daughters of Atlas were raised
to the heavens, seven loosened stars
scorched down to earth; when the seventh sister
vanished, it follows, a new star bloomed—
above Egypt, perhaps, or set in a diamond ring.
And only by outrageous miracle could divinity
clothe itself as a swan or a bull
without draining all swans or bulls of majesty,
or fall as golden rain
without dulling all other showers.

So miracles there must be, for the rain
is fine silver on the roof of a room
where a spider in shadow works her equation,
where the husband and wife wedded forty-three years,
having risen to take their medicines,
resume their places, holding hands, at the hearth,
and watch as the bodies of two logs
change to fire.

Guide to the Tomb of Ankh-mahor

As you wish, I will tell you all I know.
As you wish, it will not be enough.
Remember Napoleon stumbling white and wide-eyed
from his night in the pharaoh's pyramid?
You wouldn't, if he'd obligingly blabbed his vision.
(If vision it was, as we all hope;
true, the man was known to have a weak stomach,
and the smell of bat in those oven chambers—well.)

This, of course, is no king's last mystery,
only a minor tomb of a minor official—
Supervisor of Works, Scribe of the Court,
Lord of the Secrets—whose children fondly thought
he would live forever. His reputation, I mean.
Instead, we reveal only ourselves by guessing
whether this Ankh-mahor was the nearly perfect man
depicted on these walls. Step inside,

out of the wind, the famous five-thousand-year-long
        Egyptian wind
that polishes the rough and pits the smooth,
but please try not to shuffle: dust lingers here.
Hold your wet bandannas over your mouths
and noses; proceed to the right.
The funerary reliefs you'll see
are remarkably vivid and well preserved,
and typical in their enigmatic subjects.

Note the powerful torso, the godlike eyes.
The inhabitant of the tomb is never shown
discharging his actual duties; here
he participates in a dangerous hippo hunt
that may have religious meaning,
as may the border of crocodiles.
Off to the side, in a common motif,
Ankh-mahor's servants force-feed nineteen geese.

Here he hauls in bird nets, filled with
small birds, fish, a leopard, and several
captured foreign soldiers. In the next scene,
he watches goldsmiths draw an ingot
through a series of smaller and smaller holes
to make gold wire. Beneath a damaged inscription,
in which he seems to say, ". . . brings light to my eyes . . . ,"
he inspects a tray of pastries.

On this wall Ankh-mahor stands justified
and fearless before Ma'at, Feather of Truth;
the hieroglyphs refer to "the Turquoise Ones," the gods:
"He feels their [or, gives them] pleasure."
Yet the facing relief is a simple family scene—
while a puppy chews on a ball, or perhaps an onion,
Ankh-mahor regards his wife with love.
Their three grown daughters come just to the height
    of his knee.

They appear again, this diminished generation,
in these scenes of ritual mourning. While their mother
tends the upright corpse with dignity,
they flood their hands with tears.
Implausible numbers of mourners are depicted in great detail,
including Nubians, Semites, Persians, even
        this gray-faced Greek.
Reluctantly they laud the early opening
of the double doors of Heaven.

A peculiar feature of this tomb, as you may know,
is the series of later reliefs in this passage—
unfinished, uncolored, merely outlined in rust-red,
inferior in execution.
The figures have narrower shoulders, broader hips,
and watery eyes. Their joints ache in the morning.
Apparently these are the heirs of Ankh-mahor.
They bicker. Their dog has fleas. They eat too much candy.

Instead of hunting hippos, they go fishing;
they land a few small fish and a piece of scrap metal.
One receives toxic injections around her eyes
to help maintain the classic facial expression.
In a somewhat less decadent scene,
the heirs have gathered, releasing birds.
One holds a scale, one a plate of cakes,
one a musical instrument—or perhaps a kitchen utensil.

And in these shadows, hastily outlined,
a daughter sits upright in bed
beneath a few half-legible words:
". . . Corridor of Sleep . . . called his name
[or, his name was taken(?)] . . .
ceiling struck my head."
There's nothing further. No, the mummified body
itself was not discovered.

As I suggested, it makes no sense. But then
it was not put here to please us.
Please remember to use your kerchiefs.
Think of the dust we disturb in this little space,
and the dust of those here before us.
Don't worry if it grits between your teeth.
Your body rids itself of whatever you swallow,
but what you breathe, you keep.

Twenty-seventh Gilgamesh

"I've sailed the seven seas to find you.
I crossed the cold desert with a handful of water,
the hot desert barefoot. Before I left,
I made peace among the tribes.
Though the tablets that tell of you lay in fragments,
I neither slept nor ate till I could read them."
Et cetera. My husband's visitors always start this way,
bragging about themselves to flatter him. Poor dears.
By the time they've skirted the Ocean of Death,
conquered the Peaks of Forgetfulness,
and ripped through the briars around our house,
they haven't heard their praises sung
by any voice, even their own, in far too long.

This one looks like the others, too,
handsome in a broken-nosed, sweaty way,
surprised to be nervous, his thick hands clasped
between his jouncing knees.
Uncertainty slacks the muscles around his eyes,
though he scoops up three of my whortleberry muffins
before the plate meets the table. He doesn't see me
pouring his tea; he didn't come to see me.
They never do. He doesn't see
my husband either, exactly: the man
who built one ship in his life and steered it by luck
when all the world was drowning
and there was no place to run aground.

We tossed for weeks in a rotten soup
of friends and cousins, hands and feet of strangers,
floorboards, pigs, uprooted trees,
and everything else we knew. I bailed.
I made tea. I made sure
our hands touched when he took it.
Finally the broth cleared—no more hooves or roots—
and lightened beneath us. The salt on our lips
tasted different, and the sky—
never mind, I'm getting as bad
as our babbling heroes, and this one is circling
near the question he's come to ask,
as if we don't guess what it is.

The words change—this one calls it "a cure for cancer"—
but they all come to beg for the secret of cheating death.
This is when I slip out. They don't notice.
I busy myself in the kitchen, I bustle:
It's one of my little pleasures, the breeze on my face
that tells me I'm still moving. Their stories
are too sad for me, the syllables different
but the same voice crying Enkidu,
Hylas, Patroclus, Sir Gareth,
weep for Adonais, Balder is dead,
my soul, my brother, my other self,
Daddy, Daddy, where did you go,
Absalom, Absalom, my son, my son.

Too sad. I wash a cup. Still, I wonder:
How is it death never offended them
until it took their darling, their right arm,
the other so close they shared one shadow?
Until its cold spit struck their faces?
My husband never mentions this.
Gently he explains that our lives are endless
by divine decree, not diet, exercise,
antioxidants, or chakra crystals.
He leads our drooping guest to the window.
Beautiful view—many's the calming year
I've spent looking out myself.
"There," he says. "The rain forest.

"It could be there. No promises.
It could be anywhere you haven't tried."
"There?" the boy asks, pointing. "Or there, or there?"
"It grows where you're not looking,
and it withers where you search:
underground or high in the canopy,
twined with orchids that make you itch forever,
tended by ants whose bite is deadly.
It may be gone. While you've been away
your sons grew hungry, and their sons,
and burned a few hundred acres here and there.
Keep looking around. A man needs a hobby.
You want all the answers? You want to die of boredom?"

Some of them started off with their machetes.
We haven't heard from them since.
More, like this one, despair.
Grief has already hollowed him out;
he can almost hear it chewing.
So we tell him how to cure his sorrow.
The stories call it "the herb that restores man's youth"—
same thing. He takes a deep breath, dives to the sea floor,
single-mindedly gropes past the seaweed fungus
that might heal herpes, suspended particles
that could ease arthritis, the lethal cone snail's
cure for epilepsy, seizes a little gray plant,
and comes up dripping, more heroic already.

He wraps it in a plastic bag and goes.
As usual, he thinks he knows what he's doing.
But soon he grows tired. So do I,
despite my privileged state, thank heaven;
how else to enjoy a sleep? I lie down with my husband,
the only woman on earth unafraid
of losing half her shadow, and because I know
our hero will wake up lost, almost ordinary,
to see his herb is gone—snakes used to get them,
but nowadays it's mostly roaches, as if they needed more—
I send him the good dream, so he rolls over smiling,
the one where he's sailed five seas, and done it well,
and the best two lie ahead.

Contagion

A yawn began in Temujin, Genghis Khan.
The morning sacrifice to the mountain
    that saved his life was done.
No battle today or tomorrow. And the Chinese priest,
brought here because he might know immortality's secret,
continued to speak on every subject but that one.
The khan was strong from his time on the mountain
Burkhan Khaldun, confounding his enemies,
living on flesh of mice and marmots,
sleeping with one eye open—but so was the yawn.
It pressed the back of his throat. His nostrils flared.
Before it could force his lips open, he granted it passage.

As it swelled before him, two generals in the pavilion
received its contagion, which no one yet understands,
but they bit it back until they left his presence.
Then it pried their jaws apart,
making the eyes of all who saw them water.
All the next day, galloping west,
this and that man of the Mongol troops
carried the seed of that yawn at the root of his tongue.

Their little horses pounded the dying grass of July
beneath their hooves, but the army made no thunder;
though they were many, the land was too hard
and too wide to shake. Mushroom spores
laced the dun hills with green loops
of mysterious writing. Near dusk, the entire force
rode an hour's journey out of its way
to avoid the breath of a marmot twisting with sickness.

In summer a marmot can curse a man
with dizziness, swollen groins and armpits,
fever madness for ten days, and welcome death.

At the end of sixty miles, the army
halted. All evening among the tents
and bowls of *arkhi,* the yawn made round
the mouth of one man and shoved into another's,
stretching the space between his ears.
It never took the horses. Everyone knows
yawns are not for nervous prey, eaters of grass,
but only for killers—tigers, dogs, men.

So down the years, flooding the lands
with fear and the campaigns of the khans,
the conquering Mongols carried the yawn of Temujin
across the steppes, the feet of their many horses
raising dust above the unresonant earth,
to Turkistan, the banks of the Indus,
Azerbaijan, the Caucasus, and Russia.
Their shadows scraped over green runes in summer
and burrows of sickly marmots;
they bore a germ in the dark of their throats
from Samarkand to the Black Sea.

Ice Hotel

In winter, when the sun is reduced
to a glowworm on the horizon,
the ice hotel rises on the hardened river,
with more rooms every year, though no one
stays there more than one night.
The last living things you'll see when you enter
are plants in the lobby—
lichen and pearlwort, pink snow algae.
From shelves of ice you claim all the furs you can carry,
you put on fine boots with soles made of reindeer forehead,
and the rest is ice, even your room key,
even the lock. Your room
is a cube of frozen air with a long ice bed
and a low ice table whose lion feet
clasp balls of ice. And given that
a cup of steaming chocolate can't thaw
a patch of slush where it stands,
not your hands nor your bottom will ever
make a dent in this place, so you might as well
explore. There's only one story,
but so many rooms, so many halls—
some with dragons carved in the lintel,
some with egg-and-dart molding, acanthus
fireplaces full of ice flames,
rows of ice books, bowls of ice fruit—
that even if you go back to look for
the perfectly sculpted ice man you thought you saw
kneeling with hammer and chisel beside
an unfinished armoire, you won't find him.
The only light you have to go by

glows in the walls, twilight blue,
blue of a candle flame nearest the wick.
Back in your own blue room, you try
to warm it by being there, speaking aloud,
but your breath rises stiffly; it roughens the ceiling
with incidental stalactites.
They point to your sleep.
Later, much later, pressed by summer,
the ice hotel sinks back into river water,
adding to it a few lost car keys, pieces of paper
with words soaked away, a glove, a cup,
twists of bedding,
coins that drop in pairs from melted pillows.

Caravan with Orchids and Pearls

Gold that we are not meant to discover,
silver we found and must not keep—
without our consent or need of it,
llamas move the treasures of Earth
from place to place. And whether the look
of their overhung muzzles is scornful
or their long-lashed eyes are tender, we can't see;
they move by night. Their feet are soft
from walking on air, their panniers lumpy
with rubies, silk, lost Bach cantatas,
tiny frogs whose sweat is medicine,
and sleeping human babies.
The llamas climb shifting thermal dunes
with their clever toes. They fertilize
the world with their dung; they polish it
with their rough wool sides.
Though their only means of self-defense
is to spit in an enemy's face,
they hold their heads high.
They keep moving. Someone wakes
with empty hands she'd dreamed were full
and across the dawn sees brown clouds, heavy-laden,
already leaving her sky.

La Marée

Under the hum of the house enclosing space,
>> its mortgage paid, its roof repaired,
>> its gargoyles, lamps, and bookshelves recently
>> dusted,
under the sigh of cars crawling up the hill
>> on a road that wasn't paved when he and she
>> moved into the house with four children,
under the ripple down at the end of their yard
>> where the brown creek thumbs its crooked
>> banks,
the rustle of deer setting slim feet one at a time
>> on purple trumpets and mint in the neighbor's
>> garden
>> and chewing her spinach and roses,
then under the air-conditioned machinery silence
> of the elevator,
under the doctor's voice heavy
>> with its accustomed load of bad news,
and their own quiet voices on the way home,
they hear the rising tide

and they know the sound. They heard it
forty-two years ago on their honeymoon, as they
approached the brown ziggurat of Mont-Saint-Michel.
Their weddings, civil and church, were held in Paris
>> once they met the terms of their scholarships,
>> and school was out, and their landladies beamed,
>> and their favorite professor recorded the vows
>> on a hand-cranked machine,
>> so their voices grow lower and slower on tape

and the organ music expires at the end with
fatigue;
the Tennessee groom gazed at his Illinois bride
(and sometimes still does) as if she were
Nike of Samothrace
and the rings of Saturn and a wedge of pecan pie.
The next day at dusk when they reached the mount,
a quick vein of sea was pulsing over the
causeway, but
a cluster of locals bustled them into a flat boat, oarless,
and smiling pushed them off—

all they need do was stand in the boat facing forward,
stand in his good dark suit her good white suit
with gloves
and her little hat with its little net
and the white gold rings on their hands,
floating across fifteen yards of calm water.
They see faces leaning out of the evening.
They wait for the moment to step ashore,
to touch for balance
the outstretched hands of strangers.

Lullaby After Midnight

The tallest elephant draws night down
in a swathe that unrolls and falls and folds
on her shoulders, doubles back, doubles again,
heaping its thicknesses into pure dark.

Safe in that velvet, elephants sleep on the ground
for an hour, and kudu on buckled knees.
Birds cover their heads; dusk-hunting snakes
compose themselves around full bellies.

Baobabs sigh and stretch their roots
a further inch into earth. Where people lie still,
dreams slip between the bars of their cages.
Even the animals back of the stars come out.

Now mist-drops touch and grow heavy enough for rain.
Now babies wake their mothers from inside:
Into a place so damp and dark and quiet,
they are willing to be born.

World Truffle

This time the mycorrhizal infection
at the crooked roots of a hazelnut tree
meets a set of conditions so knotted and invisible
it feels like good will, or magic,
when the truffle begins its warty branches
that grow away from the sun.
This time it doesn't stop with one fairy ring
and dissolute spores, but fingers its way
beneath the turf and under the fence
and past the signs for Truffle Reserve:
Harvest Regulated by the State Forestry Department,
out through Umbria, up the shank of Italy;
it enmeshes the skin of the Alps.
In time its pale filaments have threaded Europe and,
almost as stubborn as death, are probing
sand on one side and burrowing on the other
through the heated muttering bed of the sea.
Its pregnant mounds rise modestly
in deserts, rain forests, city parks;
yellow truffle-flies hover and buzz
at tiny aromatic cracks in Panama and the Aleutians.
It smells like wood smoke, humus, and ore;
it smells of sex. It smells like ten thousand years.
It smells of a promise that a little tastes better than all,
that a mix and disguise is best.
Young dogs whiff it, twist in the air,
and bury their faces in loam;
tapirs and cormorants sway in its fragrance,
camels open their nostrils for it,
coatimundi and honey badgers start digging,

lemurs bark, and octopi embrace.
Humans sense nothing unusual. Yet some of them—
teachers raking leaves in Sioux City,
truck drivers stretching their legs in Ulan Bator—
take a few deep breaths and, unaware,
begin to love the world.

Notes

"Olduvai Gorge Thorn Tree": Olduvai Gorge in Tanzania is famous for the discovery there of early hominids and their tools.

"Mount Clutter": The Ordovician is the period from 495 million to 443 million years ago. Crinoids are marine invertebrates, of which fossils are common; stromatolites are mounded bacterial mats and have also been found as fossils. Of *Insolicorypha psygma,* of the Cambrian period just preceding the Ordovician, a single fossilized specimen has been identified in the deposits of the Burgess Shale. The "razor" of William of Occam is the axiom that when one analyzes a subject, one eliminates all unnecessary facts.

"Beethoven and the Ichthyosaurs": "Must it be? . . . It must be" is printed at the beginning of the last movement of Beethoven's string quartet Opus 135. The variously interpreted fossils eventually given Latin names are all of ichthyosaurs.

"Bone Hunters in Patagonia": J. B. Hatcher and O. A. Peterson hunted fossils in South America from 1896 to 1899.

"Mound Digger": A geofact is a naturally occurring form that may appear to be made by human agency.

"Siberian Triangle": The great mathematician did in fact propose such a project. The property of density states that between any two points is another point.

"Mawson's Pie": Edgeworth David led Alistair Mackay and Douglas Mawson on an arduous but successful expedition to locate the South Magnetic Pole in 1908. Later, on an

Antarctic mapping expedition, Mawson was the hero and sole survivor of another three-man team.

"A Map of the Bufo Islands" and **"Aiaia"**: Unlike many of the animals on these fictional islands, the opabinia did exist, according to the evidence of the Burgess Shale.

"Neoteny": The term refers to the retention of immature characteristics, such as disproportionately large eyes, which adults often find attractive in babies.

"Morning on Despina": French naturalist Jean-Henri Fabre lured processional caterpillars onto the lip of a jar, brushed away the threads that led them there, and discovered that they would march in circles till exhausted.

"Ameldonia": After the island Krakatau, or Krakatoa, nearly obliterated itself in a volcanic eruption, the first life-form to be observed on it was a spider. *Umm al-duniyâ* means "mother of the world" in Arabic.

"Contagion": The theory has been proposed that the Black Plague was brought to Europe by attacking Mongols. The disease apparently strikes marmots, too.

"Lullaby After Midnight": Elephants usually sleep on their feet, but may lie down in the deep of night when they feel particularly safe. Widely accepted anecdotal evidence has it that more women go into labor at night than do during the day.

"World Truffle": No one knows yet how to initiate the growth of truffles, but it requires the infection of tree roots by mycorrhizal spores.